# Annuals

# Instant Colour

## Richard Bird

HERMES
HOUSE

The edition published by Hermes House

© Anness Publishing Limited 2002 updated 2003..

Hermes House is an imprint of Anness Publishing Limited,
Hermes House, 88–89 Blackfriars Road, London SE1 8HA

Publisher: Joanna Lorenz
Production Controller: Joanna King

Publisher's Note:
The Reader should not regard the recommendations, ideas and techniques
expressed and described in this book as substitutes for the advice of a
qualified medical practitioner or other qualified professional.
Any use to which the recommendations, ideas and techniques
are put is at the reader's sole discretion and risk.

Printed in Hong Kong/China

3 5 7 9 10 8 6 4

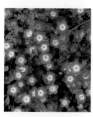

# CONTENTS

# Introduction

WHEN A GARDEN IS IN NEED OF AN INSTANT FACE-LIFT, ANNUALS ARE THE PERFECT ANSWER. THEY PROVIDE A COLOURFUL DISPLAY OVER A LONG PERIOD, YET BEING TEMPORARY, THEY ALLOW YOU TO EXPERIMENT WITH DIFFERENT SCHEMES EACH YEAR.

## WHAT IS AN ANNUAL?

The simple definition of an annual is a plant that grows from seed, then flowers, sets seed and dies all within a year. However, gardening is never that simple, and several other types of plants, including short-lived perennials and tender perennials, are often treated as annuals in the garden. Biennials are a related group which also need to be replaced, but their life cycle takes two years to complete.

## BIENNIALS AND TENDER PERENNIALS

Unlike annuals, biennials are sown in one year, planted out in the autumn and flower during the following year, usually in spring or early summer. Short-lived perennials are plants, such as snapdragons and pansies, which flower best in their first year and so are normally discarded and replaced, but they can have their flowering stems removed in order to produce flowers again in the following

**Above:** *A mixture of annuals in a large bedding scheme. Such designs can be scaled down for the small garden.*

*Above: Tender perennials are often treated as annuals. Here both dahlias and verbenas belong to this group.*

summer. Tender perennials are plants, such as geraniums and dahlias, which cannot be overwintered outside in colder climates. These can be kept indoors over winter, but many people prefer to replace them, particularly when using them as bedding plants.

### HARDINESS

Annuals are also categorized according to their hardiness. Hardy annuals are those that can be sown outside in

autumn or spring. Half-hardy annuals will not tolerate frost and are usually sown indoors for planting out when the frosts are over. Those that grow quickly enough, however, can be sown outside at the end of spring for flowering that summer. Tender annuals need to be sown in a greenhouse to ensure a long enough growing season – again, they are planted out when there is no danger of frost.

| POPULAR BIENNIALS |
| :---: |
| *Campanula medium* |
| *Dianthus barbatus* |
| *Digitalis purpurea* |
| *Erysimum (Cheiranthus)* |
| *Matthiola incana* |
| *Oenothera biennis* |
| *Silybum marianum* |
| *Verbascum* |

| POPULAR TENDER PERENNIALS |
| :---: |
| *Alcea rosea* |
| *Alonsoa warscewicizii* |
| *Antirrhinum majus* |
| *Argyranthemum* |
| *Chrysanthemum* |
| *Felicia amelloides* |
| *Dahlia* |
| *Impatiens* |
| *Pelargonium* |
| *Salvia splendens* |
| Semperflorens begonias |
| *Verbena* x *hybrida* |

*Above: Honesty,* Lunaria annua, *is a versatile, self-sowing biennial.*

## VALUE FOR MONEY

The great thing about annuals is their value for money. Many are easy to raise from seed, which can be highly rewarding. Indeed, with those hardy annuals that can be sown in situ, growing them from seed is scarcely any more trouble than buying plants. Some are more difficult to germinate, but small plants can often be bought very cheaply, and in most cases they will flower for a long period, often from late spring right through to the first frosts of winter.

## VARIETY

Annuals have a wide range of attributes which mean that they can be used and appreciated in a number of ways. Colour is obviously one of their main qualities. This can be from dazzling reds to very subtle pinks and blues. Some have very colourful or shapely leaves and are used as foliage plants, others have a mixture of both attractive flowers and foliage. Many have delicious scents – you only have to think of sweet peas or heliotropes.

## ANNUALS IN THE GARDEN

There are many situations in the garden where annuals are useful. One of their most popular uses is as container plants. They are perfect for containers of all sorts, from hanging baskets and window boxes to a wide variety of pots, tubs and troughs. They are also frequently used as bedding plants, either in a random, informal way for a cottage-style effect, or in traditional formal bedding schemes with geometrical designs. Some annuals have a more limited flowering period and these tend to mix in with perennials very well. Some gardeners grow annuals in separate beds, often in the vegetable garden, specifically for cutting to use in flower arranging, or for exhibition purposes.

*Left: Annuals are great in containers. They are colourful, long flowering and not difficult to look after.*

## HOW TO USE THIS BOOK

This book will introduce you to a wide range of annuals, all of which are relatively easy to grow and will definitely enhance your garden, whether it be simply confined to a couple of hanging baskets or an area the size of a soccer pitch. As well as firing your enthusiasm, there is also plenty of practical information. In *Getting Started with Annuals* you will find techniques for producing good quality plants as well as planting out and looking after your specimens. Once you have your plants it is time to think about what to do with them. *Using Annuals Effectively* suggests various ways of planting, and then some aesthetic aspects of design are addressed, as the uses of different

*Above: Trailing petunias are perfect for hanging baskets, and combine well with red geraniums and busy Lizzies.*

colours and their combinations are considered. In this handbook you will find all you need to know to create a beautiful display of colourful plants that will give you and your friends pleasure throughout the summer.

*Above: There would not be bedding without annuals. The even height and vivid colour of these geraniums makes them perfect for use in such schemes.*

7

# Getting Started with Annuals

ANNUALS ARE NOT DIFFICULT PLANTS TO GROW, BUT IT IS A GOOD
IDEA TO LEARN A FEW SIMPLE TECHNIQUES BEFORE YOU START. THIS
WILL HELP ENSURE THE SUCCESS OF YOUR EFFORTS, AS WELL AS
MAKING THEM MORE REWARDING.

## ACQUIRING PLANTS

There are basically two ways of obtaining annuals: growing them from seed or buying plants. Seed is cheaper, and there is also a wider range of colours and varieties to choose from. Additionally, there is a great sense of satisfaction if you have the time to raise plants yourself. However, if you simply want to save time and effort, you can buy plants – either tiny ones that will need potting on, or larger specimens that are ready to plant out.

## SOWING SEEDS INDOORS

With half-hardy and tender annuals, the seeds are best sown indoors in pots or modular trays, and planted out when the weather is warm enough. Hardy annuals can be sown outside, but with some varieties you may choose to sow them indoors to give them an earlier start. Check the seed packet for the correct sowing time for each variety. Take care, particularly with very fine seeds, not to sow them too thickly – if overcrowded they will not grow well, and will also be difficult to separate without damaging them.

**1** Fill the pot with compost (soil mix) to 1cm (½in) below the rim, water and scatter the seeds thinly and evenly on the surface. Larger seeds should be well spaced and buried slightly below the surface. Alternatively, sow the seeds in a modular tray allowing one or two seeds per cell. This will avoid root disturbance later.

**2** Unless the seed is very fine, cover with about 5mm of fine grit. This will prevent the surface compacting, allowing for more even watering. It also keeps the neck of the seedlings dry, preventing rotting.

**3** Place the pot in a warm greenhouse or propagator or on a warm windowsill, but not in direct sunlight. Keep the pots watered. Once the seeds have germinated, make sure they get plenty of light.

*Above: Nasturtiums can be sown directly in the ground or will self-sow.*

## SOWING DIRECTLY IN THE GROUND

Hardy annuals can be sown directly outside. Ensure that the soil is weed-free, finely raked and well watered. You can simply scatter the seed where it is to flower, raking it over lightly. If you prefer, make a shallow drill and sow the seed in this, before covering it over. If you are not sure what your seedlings will look like, this method will help you to identify them when weeding. You can then move them to their final position when large enough. Keep the seedlings watered in dry weather.

### SELF-SOWING

After flowering, many annuals, such as poppies, nasturtiums, honesty and love-in-a-mist, will self-sow freely. They can be simply left to flower year after year, thinning them out or moving them as necessary.

### BUYING PLANTS

Choose plants that look healthy and vigorous, and free of insect pests. If you can remove them from the pots, check that the roots are not pot-bound. They should look well-cared-for – not overcrowded, and neither dry nor standing in a lot of water.

---

### GARDENER'S TIP

Label each pot before you sow the seed as it is very easy to forget what is in each pot once the seed is sown.
Continue to label individual pots once the seedlings have been pricked out, especially if there are several different colours of the same plant.
When watering, it is often best to stand the pots in water until the surface feels moist, rather than watering from above, which can disturb the delicate seedlings.

---

*Above: Lobelias are easy to grow from seed and will reward you with a mass of colourful flowers that are ideal for edging or hanging baskets.*

## PRICKING OUT

When your seedlings are large enough to handle, usually when they have produced their second pair of leaves, they can be pricked out. This means transplanting them, either into individual pots or into trays, with plenty of space to allow them to grow. Do not let the seedlings grow too big before doing this, or they may become drawn through overcrowding.

**1** Water the plants several hours before pricking out. Half-fill a pot with a good quality potting compost (soil mix), then remove the seedlings from their pot. Rather than trying to dig them out, remove the whole rootball – as well as being easier, this is less likely to damage the roots.

**2** Holding a seedling by one of its lower leaves, suspend it in the pot and carefully trickle more compost around the roots. Gently firm the compost around the roots. The final soil level around the seedling should be the same as it was in the original pot or tray.

**3** Tap the pot gently on the table to settle the compost around the seedling and water carefully. Watering from below by standing the pot in water until the surface is moist will avoid disturbing the seedling.

**4** To plant seedlings in trays, fill with compost, firm down gently, and make holes with your finger or a dibber. Insert the plants, firming the compost gently around them, and water from below.

### GARDENER'S TIP

Seedlings should always be handled by their leaves rather than the stems or roots, as slight damage to the leaves is less likely to be fatal to the plants.

## PREPARING THE YOUNG PLANTS

The plants can be allowed to grow on in a greenhouse or cold frame until they are ready to plant out. Any half-hardy and tender annuals should not be planted out until after the frosts have passed, which usually means early summer. Do not take the plants straight from the greenhouse and plant them out. They should first be hardened off, or gently acclimatized to the outside temperatures. At first place them outside or open the cold frame for an hour or so each day, gradually increasing the time until they are permanently in the open air. They are then ready to plant out.

## PREPARING THE GROUND

It is important both with plants grown from seed and with bought plants to offer them a well-prepared bed. Dig the soil over in the previous autumn, removing all weeds and adding in

*Above: When planting up a hanging basket, standing it on a large pot or bucket will help to keep it stable.*

plenty of well-rotted organic material, such as garden compost or farmyard manure. In the spring rake this over and break it down into a fine tilth, at the same time removing any weeds that have appeared since it was dug.

## PLANTING OUT

Tease out the roots gently before planting. This is particularly important in the open ground, as the roots may be reluctant to move from the soft potting compost (soil mix) into heavier soil. The plants should be planted in the ground or in their container at the same depth as they were in their pots. Firm the soil or potting compost then water in.

*Above: Digging over the soil, removing weeds and incorporating well-rotted farmyard manure or compost will give your new plants a good start.*

---

### GARDENER'S TIP

Do not plant the young plants too close to each other, allow them room to grow. Aim just to cover the ground by the time they are mature.

---

# Annuals Maintenance

ANNUALS ARE NOT DIFFICULT TO LOOK AFTER, AND CAN BE ONE OF THE MOST TROUBLE-FREE ELEMENTS OF THE GARDEN. HOWEVER, THERE ARE A FEW BASIC TASKS THAT MUST BE ATTENDED TO, PARTICULARLY WITH PLANTS IN CONTAINERS.

## WATERING

Perhaps the most important task that needs to be undertaken is the watering of the plants. All plants need water to survive. Many bedding plants are tolerant of drought conditions, but in most cases they will perform less well. Below the surface the soil often contains a reserve of moisture, and so plants in the open ground can usually survive for surprisingly long periods of dry weather, but plants in containers must be watered regularly, often more than once a day in hot weather. Even if it does rain, the water often runs off the leaves when containers are closely planted, and fails to reach the roots.

### Watering Aids

There are various simple ways to reduce the necessity for frequent watering. In the open ground, adding organic material such as garden compost to the soil will help it to retain moisture, and mulching with a layer of such material on the surface will reduce

*Right: Plants in containers need regular watering. Make sure you water thoroughly, until the water starts to come out of the drainage holes at the bottom.*

evaporation. With containers, you can add moisture-retaining gels or granules to the compost (soil mix) before planting, or use special container compost which already includes this. (Do not add more than the recommended amount as it can expand and froth out.) You can also buy 'self-watering' containers, with a reservoir which allows you to water less frequently.

### Watering

For containers and individual plants, a watering can is the easiest method. For large areas of open ground, or large numbers of containers, a hose is easier

– hand-held with a spray attached, or static with a sprinkler or dribble hose. (Sprinklers lose a lot of water through evaporation, so a dribble hose is preferable.) Watering in the evening will reduce the loss through evaporation. Make sure you water thoroughly – an occasional soaking is much better than little and often, which can encourage the growth of shallow roots just below the surface.

## FEEDING

Annuals planted in the open ground will rarely need feeding, unless the soil is very poor. Indeed, many will actually flower better in poor soil, merely growing more leafy if over-fed. In containers, however, plants generally do need feeding, since they are usually closely planted in a very limited volume of compost (soil mix), and the nutrients in the compost will all have washed away after a few weeks of frequent watering.

*Above: Slow-release fertilizers, available in either granules or plugs, can be added to the compost in containers.*

### Types of Fertilizer

Fertilizer in granular or liquid form can be added to the soil or compost when watering. Always follow the manufacturer's instructions. Liquid seaweed extract is an organic alternative. Liquid types can also be applied as a foliar spray, for more rapid absorption if the plants are very starved. With plants in containers, you can use slow-release fertilizers, available in granular or plug form. These are simply added to the compost and will remain effective throughout the season, avoiding the need for regular feeding.

*Above: For carpet bedding and borders a dribble hose saves time, but be certain to water thoroughly.*

## GENERAL MAINTENANCE

Most annuals will perform well with little or no physical maintenance, but some types do require help. With almost all, you will find that a little extra attention will improve the display, and ensure that it lasts as long as possible.

*Above:* Push the supports firmly into the soil so that the hoop is about halfway up the eventual height of the plant.

*Above:* Linked stakes provide an effective support, and will not be visible once covered by the plants.

## Staking

Most annuals are now available in short forms that do not need staking. However, sometimes it is desirable to have tall plants, and many varieties will need supports of some kind. Individual stems can be supported by being tied to canes. Large clumps can be grown through special hoops or systems of linked stakes that are sold for this purpose. Alternatively, for a more natural look, use peasticks or brushwood pushed into the ground around the plants, with a mesh of string tied between the sticks if necessary.

## Pinching Out and Disbudding

When new plants are first planted it is a good idea to pinch out the leading shoot. This will encourage the plant to develop side-shoots and become bushy. If you want to grow specimen flowers, then it may be necessary to reduce the number so that energy is concentrated in those remaining. The flower buds on the minor stems can be removed, leaving just those at the tip of the shoots to develop.

## Deadheading and Cutting Back

Take off flowerheads as they die, as this will promote prolonged flowering as well as making the plant look neater. At the same time cut back any stems that are becoming too long or have finished flowering. New shoots will generally appear to replace them.

## TAKING CUTTINGS

A number of the tender perennials, such as geraniums, and many short-lived perennials can be over-wintered for the following year by taking cuttings in the late summer or autumn.

**1** Using a sharp knife or secateurs (pruners) cut a short length of healthy, non-flowering shoot, just below a leaf joint. Cut off the lower leaves close to the stem, just leaving a few at the top.

**2** Fill a pot with good quality cutting compost (soil mix) or standard compost mixed with grit for extra drainage. Plant the cuttings around the edge of the pot.

**3** Water them and cover the pot with a plastic bottle or plastic bag, or place in a propagator, to reduce water loss. Keep them out of direct sunlight.

**4** When the cuttings have rooted and new growth has appeared, the plants can be potted on into individual pots. Keep them indoors over winter.

### GARDENER'S TIP
When taking cuttings, put them in a plastic bag to keep them fresh until you need them.

*Above: Once a multi-stemmed plant is established, pinch out the top growth to encourage a bushier shape.*

15

## WEEDING

However carefully you clear the ground before planting, new weeds will inevitably appear. They not only look untidy, but compete with your annuals for water, nutrients and light. The best way to control them in planted areas is by hand weeding, removing the roots if possible, or regular hoeing.

If perennial weeds are amongst your plants, and you cannot uproot them without disturbing other roots, just remove the top growth regularly – if this is done at least once a week, they will eventually weaken and die. You can try killing them using a glyphosate-based gel that is brushed on to the leaves, but be careful not to get any on the other plants. Applying a mulch of composted bark, or simply planting close together so that little light reaches the ground, will help prevent weed seeds germinating.

*Above: If the established plants are not too big then it is possible to hoe between them using a long- or short-handled hoe. Be careful that you do not cut down the plants as well.*

*Above: A thick mulch of composted bark will effectively suppress germination of weed seeds, though if any perennial weed roots are in the soil they will still come through.*

*Above: Try to get all the weed roots out, if you can do so without disturbing the roots of nearby plants.*

### GARDENER'S TIP
Try to weed the garden regularly, so that weeds do not have a chance to grow very large and develop established roots. This makes the job much easier.

## DISEASES AND PESTS

If your plants are given good conditions and are growing vigorously, they may well suffer no problems, particularly if you choose resistant varieties. Looking to see which plants grow well in other gardens in your area is a good guide. However, problems may still occur.

### Diseases

Annuals are not prone to many diseases, but they may suffer powdery mildew if conditions are too dry or too wet, particularly if air circulation is poor. Thinning the plants may help, but remove and destroy any badly affected growth. You can treat mildew and other fungal diseases with a chemical spray, but it tends to occur late in the season, when the annuals will soon be over anyway.

### Pests

Aphids are a common insect pest, and they can be killed using an aphid-specific spray, but often this is not necessary as the attack is only temporary. Slugs, snails and caterpillars can do a lot of damage to seedlings and newly-planted plants. Slugs and snails can be killed with a chemical bait, but this can harm wildlife and pets. An effective biological control is also available for slugs, though not snails. Alternatively, you can go out at night with a flashlight and rubber gloves, and collect slugs and snails, or sink saucers of beer in the ground, which will attract

*Above: Snails can cause devastation in the border as they are partial to tender young shoots. They are mainly active at night, so you can catch them then.*

*Above: Caterpillars can demolish succulent leaves and flowers in only a few hours. Rub the yellow eggs off leaves as soon as you see them.*

and drown them. If you have a pond, the frogs will eat large quantities of these pests. Caterpillars are best controlled by looking for their yellow eggs on leaves in the early evening, and rubbing them off.

# Using Annuals Effectively

THE TEMPORARY NATURE OF ANNUALS MAKES THEM IDEAL PLANTS
FOR EXPERIMENTING WITH INTERESTING EFFECTS. IT IS WORTH TRYING
OUT UNUSUAL COMBINATIONS OF COLOUR AND FORM – IF YOU ARE
NOT HAPPY WITH THE RESULTS YOU CAN CHANGE THEM NEXT YEAR.

## GETTING THE CONDITIONS RIGHT

Many of the annuals grown in gardens are reasonably tolerant of a wide range of conditions, though most will perform best in a sunny, well-drained site. If your soil is very heavy, you can improve the drainage by adding plenty of horticultural grit or sand – this is especially helpful in a very wet or sunless site which might be prone to waterlogging. Shade is more difficult to counteract – light shade is fine for most annuals, but if it is very deep shade, you will be limited in your choice of plants. Foxgloves, for example, may succeed, and busy Lizzies are also worth trying – they are one of the few plants that will give a really colourful show in a shady spot, yet they are also happy in sun.

**Above:** *Some annuals self-sow freely once they have flowered. Here, they have sown themselves a little too closely together, but if thinned out they should flower again with no further attention.*

**Above:** *These sweet Williams are a mixture of colours that harmonize together very well. Care would be needed when adding other plants to the scheme, so as not to spoil the effect.*

18

## GETTING THE SCHEME RIGHT

Annuals are versatile plants. You may choose to use them simply as flowering plants mixed in with perennials in the border – this can be a good way to create a cottage-garden effect, particularly if you allow the plants to self-sow randomly. They can also be used as temporary fillers in a more planned mixed border.

Many gardeners, on the other hand, prefer to create bedding schemes made up entirely of annuals, and this is an ideal way to create a formal design. Whichever way you want to use annuals, their ephemeral nature means that you can try out a different scheme each year. Since annuals offer such a wide range of bold, bright colours, as well as more delicate, subtle ones, there is plenty of scope for imaginative self-expression.

## GETTING THE PLANTS RIGHT

If you want to make things easy for yourself, particularly if you are new to gardening, you will probably do well to choose from the many plants that are widely available in garden centres, or those that you see flourishing in other people's gardens. The reason for their popularity is usually their reliability – often these are the plants that will flower for a long period, suffering few problems. However, you may wish to be more adventurous. Seed catalogues will offer a far wider range

***Above:*** *This delightful spring border, combining deep blue forget-me-nots and pink daisies with delicate tulips, shows a careful use of colour while still creating an attractively informal effect.*

of plants, so if you grow from seed you will be able to create more interesting and unusual effects. Some of the less common plants may have shorter flowering periods, but you can allow for this when planning your scheme. If you do not want to raise seeds, try mail-order plant suppliers – many of these will produce a wider range than you can find at most garden centres.

19

## BEDDING SCHEMES

Many annuals, particularly the smaller varieties, will grow very uniformly in terms of height, size and colour. These are ideal for bedding schemes where blocks or patterns are required.

*Above: This design has been created entirely from foliage plants, showing that different leaf colours can produce an effect as striking as flowers.*

The possibilities for creativity here are endless – it is a good idea to visit public parks and gardens for inspiration, particularly if you want to make a traditional, formal scheme. However, there is no need to restrict yourself to traditional patterns. Geometrical shapes can also be used in new and striking ways, or you may want to create a softer effect, perhaps with swirling lines or colours subtly merging into one another. If your design contains intricate details, make sure you choose only small, neat plants that will suit the scheme.

## COLOUR AND TEXTURE

Bedding plants can be used almost like a paintbox – indeed, you might even find inspiration for your design by visiting an art gallery for colour ideas, as well as the more obvious approach of wandering around garden centres looking at different plants and placing them together to see how they combine. Do not overlook the value of foliage plants – many bedding plants are grown purely for their foliage, and these are often silver-leaved, with interesting furry textures. There are also some with deep red or purple leaves, or variegated plants such as coleus, with many colour variations.

*Above: Large triangular blocks of colour, here using geraniums and busy Lizzies in shades of pink and purple, create a vivid impact in this border.*

### GARDENER'S TIP

Remember that the smaller and neater the plants you use, the more detailed and intricate your design can be.

## INFILLING WITH COLOUR

Blocks of colours can be used to fill in shapes within an outline, which can be 'drawn' either with a single variety of small annual – foliage plants are often a good choice – or with a line of permanent small hedging plants such as box. The latter is the classic method for creating a traditional parterre. Though this will be a permanent feature, you will still be able to vary the annuals that are planted within the shapes.

## VARYING THE HEIGHT

Plants of different heights can be used to great effect in bedding schemes. You need to be careful with detailed patterns – if taller plants are hiding smaller ones the effect can be spoiled. However, by grading the heights so that taller plants

*Above: A neatly clipped box parterre with a filling of summer plants. When these are finished they will be replaced by colourful winter pansies.*

are towards the back of a border, or in the centre of an island bed, you can create a design that still looks very neat and regular while gaining extra interest from the added vertical dimension.

## CREATING THE DESIGN

It is often difficult to imagine how a scheme will look when it is planted out, and it can be helpful to draw it on paper first, using crayons or coloured pencils. If you make your drawing to scale, you can also use it to work out how many plants you are likely to need – this is particularly useful if you are covering a large area.

21

## MIXING IT

Many of the annuals work well in a mixed border with perennials, in an informal cottage-garden style. This is particularly good for more subtle and unobtrusive flowers, such as the soft blue or white love-in-a-mist, or toad-flax in various delicate colours. These also have short flowering seasons, making them less suitable for bedding schemes, but in an informal border they can come and go, and can be allowed to self-sow. It is less easy to fit in some of the more strongly-coloured annuals, such as busy Lizzies, so choose your plants carefully.

*Above: The pale pink shades of* Cleome *blend in well with the perennials in this mixed border.*

*Above: The temporary gaps between these young shrubs are being planted with nasturtiums, which will soon spread out and fill the space.*

## TEMPORARY FILLERS

Annuals are perfect candidates for filling gaps in a border. If for example you have just planted a number of shrubs, then it will be several years before they have filled their allotted space and during that time the gaps can be filled by annuals. In the perennial border, early season plants finish flowering and their remains, often unattractive, can be hidden by planting annuals in front of them. Winter annuals can be used to fill beds that will be planted up permanently in the following spring. Filling temporary gaps with annuals not only improves the appearance of the garden, avoiding boring expanses of bare soil, but the plants can also act as a useful ground cover, especially if planted relatively close together. This will reduce the occurrence of weeds, as well as preventing erosion of the empty soil by the weather.

## GOING UP IN THE WORLD

There are a handful of annuals which are climbing plants, the best-known being sweet peas and nasturtiums. Some tender perennial climbers are also used as annuals, such as *Cobaea scandens* – this could also be grown in a tub and overwintered indoors. Climbers can be used to scramble up through other plants, perhaps providing colourful blooms after the host plant's flowers have finished. They can be grown up sticks in the centre of a bedding scheme, trained up trellising or allowed to spread out to make colourful ground cover.

*Above: Climbing annuals, such as this* Ipomoea lobata, *can be used to fill vertical space in a border. They help to relieve boring flat spaces.*

*Above: No cottage garden would be complete without the delicious scent of sweet peas.*

### POPULAR ANNUAL CLIMBERS

*Asarina erubescens*
*Cobaea scandens*
*Convolvulus tricolor*
*Eccremocarpus scaber*
*Ipomoea*
*Lablab purpureus*
(syn. *Dolichos lablab*)
*Lathyrus odoratus*
*Lathyrus sativus*
*Mikania scandens*
*Rhodochiton atrosanguineum*
*Thunbergia alata*
*Tropaeolum majus*
*Tropaeolum peregrinum*

23

## GROWING IN CONTAINERS

Many annuals are ideal for containers. If you have no garden, or if you simply want to create a few bright spots around the house, you can fill window boxes, troughs, tubs and hanging baskets to produce a riot of colour that will last throughout the summer. Pots and other containers can also be used effectively in the garden, as long as they are carefully positioned so that they blend in. Patios and steps are usually the best places, and attractively weathered containers in natural materials tend to harmonize best with the surrounding plants. The choice of annuals suitable for containers is increasing all the time, particularly trailing varieties that grow over the sides of containers or hang down from baskets. As some of the cheaper containers are not very attractive, plants that will hide them can be especially helpful.

## Suitable Containers

A wide range of containers is available, varying greatly in style and price. Obviously the appearance is the most important factor, but remember that porous terracotta pots will lose more water through evaporation than plastic. There are also plastic containers with an inbuilt reservoir. If you have a roof terrace, you may need to minimize the weight, so plastic is useful here too.

> ### GARDENER'S TIP
> Always use fresh compost whenever you replant a container. Add the old compost to a border to help condition it.

*Above:* Softer coloured annuals often look better in containers when they are grouped. Here the different heights and shapes of the containers add to the interest.

## Planting Containers

Always use a good compost (soil mix). If you add a slow-release fertilizer, this will save feeding later on, and you can also mix in water-retaining granules, unless the compost already contains them. Place some drainage material in the bottom of the container – stones, broken pots or even broken polystyrene (styrofoam) plant trays are all suitable. Then fill with compost, plant the plants and water well. If the container is heavy, it may be easier to move it to its final position before filling.

## Looking After Containers

The one maintenance task that cannot be avoided is watering. Whereas plants in borders can survive periods of drought by drawing on water from deep down,

*Above:* Helichrysum *is a delightful plant for a container.*

containers do not have this resource. They can dry out very quickly in hot weather, particularly if closely planted in a small volume of compost, and may sometimes need watering more than once a day. Apart from this, and regular feeding if you do not use a slow-release fertilizer, there is little to do except occasionally removing dead flowers and straggly stems.

*Above: Assemble everything you need before you fill the container with plants. Do not forget to place a layer of drainage material at the bottom of the container. Slow-release fertilizer and water-retaining granules can be added to the compost at this stage.*

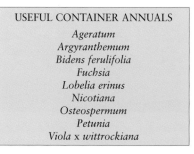

| USEFUL CONTAINER ANNUALS |
|:---:|
| *Ageratum* |
| *Argyranthemum* |
| *Bidens ferulifolia* |
| *Fuchsia* |
| *Lobelia erinus* |
| *Nicotiana* |
| *Osteospermum* |
| *Petunia* |
| *Viola* x *wittrockiana* |

## WINDOW BOXES

Annuals in window boxes are a wonderful way to brighten up your home. They not only look good from outside, but are also a lovely sight from inside the house, and can make a great difference if you do not have a garden or any other greenery to look out on. Make sure you include some upright plants as well as trailing ones if you want to have a good view of them from inside, though they may reduce the light coming through the window if they grow very tall. Always ensure that the box is secure, with no danger of it falling and possibly injuring someone below. You should also remember that it needs to be accessible for watering. If you replant the box each season, you can easily have a colourful display throughout the year.

## Planting a Window Box

Window boxes can be planted just as you would any other container. As they tend to be heavy when full, it is usually easier to place them in their final position before planting, unless this is very inconvenient. When arranging the plants, it is best to place trailing plants in front of the upright ones, or if the box is too narrow for this, simply plant them alternately in a row.

---

### WINDOW BOX ANNUALS

*Ageratum*
*Begonia*
*Brachyscome*
*Erysimum cheiri*
*Fuchsia*
*Helichrysum*
*Lobelia*
*Nicotiana*
*Sutera cordata* (*Bacopa*)
*Tagetes*

---

**Above:** *This charming stone window box is filled with yellow pansies, white lobelias and yellow and white daisies, combined with the silvery foliage of* Senecio.

## HANGING BASKETS

Nothing creates a more welcoming feeling than a colourful hanging basket or two by your front door. They can also be placed on other parts of the house, perhaps to brighten up a dull passageway, or to enhance the view from indoors. You can even use them in the garden, hanging from a fence, pergola or free-standing pole. There are plenty of suitable plants to choose from, and you can either combine a selection or try filling a basket with a single variety to create a vivid impact. Since baskets are usually heavily planted in a relatively small volume of compost, it is worth considering the type with an inbuilt reservoir, particularly if it will be in a sunny position, so that it will not dry out too quickly.

### Planting a Basket

Before you fill the basket, it needs to be lined – there are many types of liner available, including sphagnum moss, coir fibre and cardboard. You can also make a very effective liner from an old knitted woollen garment, or crochet one yourself. Place the basket on a large pot or bucket to help keep it stable. Part fill with compost, make holes in the sides of the liner and poke the roots of plants through, then continue to fill and plant more plants on the top. The compost should come up to about 2cm (1in) below the rim of

**Above:** *As well as vivid red petunias, this basket contains strawberry plants, which should produce a tasty crop later in the season. Feed regularly for a longer flowering season.*

the basket. Water the basket well and hang it securely. Keep the compost moist by watering daily or twice a day in very dry conditions.

> ### ANNUALS FOR HANGING BASKETS
> *Anagallis*
> *Asarina*
> *Bidens ferulifolia*
> *Brachyscome*
> *Diascia*
> *Felicia amelloides*
> *Fuchsia*
> *Helichrysum*
> *Lobelia*
> *Petunia*
> *Verbena*
> *Viola*

# Planning Annuals for Colour

WITH SO MANY PLANTS TO CHOOSE FROM, PLANNING A SCHEME FOR A GARDEN CAN SEEM A DAUNTING PROSPECT. HOWEVER, WITH ANNUALS YOU CAN TRY SOMETHING DIFFERENT EACH YEAR, AND YOU WILL SOON FIND OUT WHAT WORKS WELL IN TERMS OF STYLE AND COLOURING.

## COLOURFUL ANNUALS

Some of the most brightly coloured plants in the garden are annuals, and there are also plenty of more subdued and subtle varieties. In addition, many flowers contain more than one colour – pansies, for example, often have two completely different colours, and there are countless varieties that have flowers streaked or shaded with darker and paler tones. With such a wide range of plants to choose from, there is almost no limit to the effects you can create.

*Above: The rich salmon pink of this geranium, together with the size of the flowers, creates a vivid impact.*

### Moods

The colours of your plants will affect the mood of the garden. Those colours often described as 'hot', namely reds and fiery oranges, create a vibrant, lively feeling; the 'cool' blues, on the other hand, tend to produce a calming effect. Pale pastels, especially the delicate shades of pink, cream and blue, can create a soft, romantic atmosphere. Large, bold flowers will also produce a quite different mood from smaller, more unobtrusive varieties.

*Above: Stately evening primrose has tall spikes of vibrant yellow flowers that will be a focal point in a garden.*

## MIXING COLOURS

You can create many different effects in your garden by mixing colours in interesting ways. Ultimately, of course, it is a matter of personal preference, but some basic guidelines can be helpful. In general, if you want to create a dramatic, invigorating effect, choose hot colours, and strong contrasts such as blue and orange or deep purple and yellow which will catch the eye and give a sense of excitement. A whole range of different strong colours mixed together in a single area can also be very lively and cheerful, but may become wearing if used too extensively. For a quiet, restful atmosphere, on the other hand, use cooler hues, and more similar colours combined together.

### COLOUR WHEEL

Artists and gardeners have long been aware that colours have a relationship to each other and that these can be displayed in a simple wheel. On the wheel adjacent colours, blue and purple for instance, tend to combine in a

sympathetic way and are easy on the eye. Colours on opposite sides of the wheel, such as blue and orange, are contrasting and tend to jar and shock the eye. Both combinations have their uses in creating a border.

*Above: Hot yellow and red are here combined on one flower,* Ipomoea lobata. *The effect is dramatic.*

## DON'T FORGET THE FOLIAGE

We tend to think of colour in the garden in terms of flowers, with foliage, if we consider it at all, acting as the foil to the flower colours. However, even basic green leaves come in a great variety of different greens, which will play a part in the overall effect of your scheme. There are also many plants grown for their coloured foliage, which can come in a range of colours including silver, purple and red, as well as variegated. Often no less colourful than flowers, foliage alone can be very attractive.

## RED

You can be sure of creating a strong impact with a hot red. There is the pure scarlet red, and then many gradations towards orange on the one side and purple on the other, each with a completely different character, and working differently in combination with other colours. Some of the most popular red flowers are the vivid, intense reds, such as certain varieties of geranium and busy Lizzie. The effect is emphasized when the flowers are large and abundant. Poppies can also be very bright, though the black centres of the flowers, as well as their delicate papery quality, dilute the intensity.

*Above:* Dahlia *'Bishop of Llandaff'* has brilliant red flowers, made more striking by the contrast with the yellow in the centres, and the dark, purple-tinted leaves.

*Above:* Verbena *'Sandy Scarlet' cannot fail to be noticed.*

As the reds move towards purple, the effect is softened, though the colour can still be very eye-catching. Some varieties of pinks, such as *Dianthus chinensis* 'Fire Carpet', and red petunias, have just a faint touch of purple which makes the red less overpowering. The soft texture of the petunias also makes a difference, as the light will catch them at different angles, creating a variation in the red. Some sweet peas are a strong red, but their delicate shape and the paler shading towards the centre softens the effect.

## The Orange Reds

These are bright and fiery. They are very hot colours and always give a feeling of excitement and fun. They can add a lift to any colour scheme, and combine well with other hot colours, the shades of orange, orange-yellow and gold, to create a bright, summery impression. Orange reds can be overpowering if used in large quantities, but they can be toned down by including some paler shades, which will help to ensure that they are merely cheerful rather than overbearing.

The contrast with fresh green foliage can also be very effective. This is demonstrated by some of the geraniums, where the bright flowers stand out strongly against the green leaves.

*Above: This formal bedding scheme uses hot red geraniums and yellow daisies, set off by areas of purple foliage, in a bold geometrical design.*

*Above: Pelargonium 'Deacon Mandarin' is a lively choice for the garden.*

31

## The Purple Reds

These are still very intense, but more subdued and less fiery than the orange reds. They could be said to be sumptuous rather than bright. Purples and deep blues make good partners, producing a rich, opulent effect, as can be seen with the many varieties of petunia in these shades. For a more dramatic contrast, try combining them with orange.

## WHERE TO USE REDS

Reds can be used wherever you want to make a strong statement. Many of the red annuals, particularly the more intense ones, tend to be more successful when used in bedding schemes and containers, rather than in mixed borders. The vivid red geraniums, verbenas and busy Lizzies are enormously popular plants for window boxes and other containers, and are guaranteed to draw

*Above: Busy Lizzies are excellent for brightening up a dull, shady area, as they are one of the few red-flowered plants that will tolerate shade. They work well in containers or as bedding.*

the eye. Poppies seem to fit in more easily with an informal scheme, and indeed they have long been a favourite

---

GORGEOUS RED ANNUALS

*Adonis aestivalis*
*Alcea rosea* 'Scarlet'
*Cosmos bipinnatus* 'Pied Piper Red'
*Dianthus chinensis* 'Fire Carpet'
*Impatiens* Tempo Burgundy
*Lathyrus odoratus*
'Winston Churchill'
*Linum grandiflorum*
*Lobelia erinus* 'Rosamund'
*Papaver rhoeas*
*Pelargonium* (many red varieties)
*Petunia* 'Mirage Velvet'
*Salvia splendens*
Semperflorens begonia
*Tagetes patula* 'Scarlet Sophie'
*Verbena* 'Blaze'

---

*Above: Love-lies-bleeding bears long panicles of deep purplish-crimson flowers. Its bushy habit makes it ideal for an informal border.*

choice for cottage gardens. They also blend in perfectly with the other more subdued flowers in a wildflower garden. The purple reds can be blended into a mixed scheme more easily than the really fiery reds, and they will combine more happily with softer pinks and blues.

*Above: A classic use of red geraniums. It is simplicity itself but it is very effective, with the terracotta pots making a perfect foil to the flowers.*

## Reds in the Shade

In a shady spot, red can take on a very deep and intense quality, with some of the brightness taken away – the crimsons and purple reds in particular are very effective. Unfortunately, there are not many red-flowered plants that are really happy in the shade, but busy Lizzies and Semperflorens begonias will grow well. In fact, as they do not like dry soil, they will often do better when out of the sun, particularly in containers, which can easily dry out.

*Above: Bright red poppies are an essential element in this wildflower garden.*

33

## ORANGE

Slightly less fiery than red, orange is still a hot colour. It has a warm, friendly feel, not as vibrant as the reds but more lively than the yellows. You can rely on it to create a cheerful atmosphere – it works especially well in window boxes and hanging baskets, where a bright focal point is required.

### Year-round Orange

Orange and the deep orange-yellows are colours of autumn – as well as the leaves on the trees, there are a number of orange flowers that appear then, such as rudbeckias and other daisies,

*Above: Pot marigolds are usually too sprawling for containers but they are excellent for adding orange to traditional cottage garden borders.*

*Below: Seen at close quarters,* Calceolaria *has a curious, delicate shape. At a distance, the mass of flowers can create bold strokes of orange.*

and also chrysanthemums. However, there are also plenty of annuals for earlier in the year, the best-known being the various types of marigolds, as well as Californian poppies. There are even orange varieties of winter-flowering pansies.

### Contrasts

If you want a strong contrast, mix oranges with blues. A much more sympathetic colouring, although still contrasting, is to have them displayed against a strong green background. Marigolds against a green hedge, for example, can look quite stunning.

A less conventional mixing would be with deep green crinkly leaved parsley. Bronze foliage can also provide a good background against which

*Above:* As well as producing striking orange flowers, cannas come in many varieties with different coloured foliage – these are a dramatic deep purple.

*Above:* There is a great range of dahlias from bright yellow through orange to almost white. They make excellent bedding plants.

to see oranges at their best. This works especially well with the more fiery oranges that are near reds.

### Orange in the Shade

There are not many orange annuals that will be happy growing in shade, but busy Lizzies and Semperflorens begonias are both available in orange varieties and these should do well. The orange colour is a good choice for a slightly gloomy spot, as it will look bright and cheerful. You can also try orange pansies, if the shade is not too deep, especially if there is some sun for part of the day.

---

**BRIGHT ORANGE ANNUALS**

*Alonsoa warscewiczii*
*Antirrhinum majus* (various varieties)
*Calceolaria* (various varieties)
*Calendula officinalis*
(various varieties)
*Emilia javanica*
*Erysimum* (*Cheiranthus*) 'Fire King'
*Eschscholzia californica*
*Helichrysum bracteatum*
(various varieties)
*Impatiens* 'Mega Orange Star'
*Mimulus* (various varieties)
*Nemesia* 'Orange Prince'
*Rudbeckia hirta* (various varieties)
*Tagetes erecta* (various varieties)
*Tithonia rotundifolia* 'Torch'
*Tropaeolum majus* (various varieties)
*Zinnia* (various varieties)

## Yellow

Like most colours yellow has two aspects. One is mixed with varying amounts of orange to produce the golds and the other contains green and is of a more lemony colour. The golds are hot or at least warm colours; the lemon yellows, by contrast, are much cooler. Although the two styles of yellow can be mixed it is usually considered better to keep them apart. In the middle is cheerful pure yellow.

### Golds

The hot golds are, like the fiery reds, quite exciting colours and can be used to uplift the spirits – it is difficult to feel low when surrounded by golden yellow flowers. It is the colour of

*Above: Golden yellow French marigolds are valuable bedding plants, especially for schemes where even height and colour are required.*

sunshine and gaiety. Containers or beds of gold will always be warming. They may not be quite so exciting as fiery red, but the colour is easier to live with. Golds mix well with other glowing colours such as the hot reds or oranges. White and gold can be very effective when used for a whole border. For a strong contrast, try combining gold and blue – the effect can be quite dramatic.

---

### BLAZING YELLOW ANNUALS

*Alcea rosea* 'Yellow'
*Anoda cristata* 'Buttercup'
*Antirrhinum majus* (yellow varieties)
*Argemone mexicana*
*Argyranthemum frutescens*
'Jamaica Primrose'
*Calendula officinalis* 'Kablouna'
*Chrysanthemum segetum*
*Cladanthus arabicus*
*Coreopsis* 'Sunray'
*Glaucium flavum*
*Helianthus annuus*
*Limnanthes douglasii*
*Limonium sinuatum*
'Forever Moonlight'
*Limonium sinuatum* 'Goldcoast'
*Lonas annua*
*Mentzelia lindleyi*
*Mimulus* (various varieties)
*Sanvitalia procumbens*
*Tagetes erecta* (yellow varieties)
*Tagetes patula* (yellow varieties)
*Tripleurospermum inodora*
'Gold Pompoms'
*Tripleurospermum inodora*
'Santana Lemon'
*Tropaeolum majus*
*Tropaeolum peregrinum*
*Viola* x *wittrockiana*
(yellow varieties)

---

## Lemons and Pale Yellows

The lemon yellows are much cooler than the golds, and these mix well with softer colours. When teamed with blue, the effect can be quite refreshing. A lemon, blue and white border can look delightfully fresh throughout the season.

*Above: The poached-egg plant self-sows in profusion, creating a brilliant display.*

## Yellows in the Shade

There are few suitable plants, but Semperflorens begonias come in yellow varieties, and pansies will also tolerate some shade.

*Above: These little chrysanthemums produce a sprawling mass of colour, perfect for an informal border. The yellow looks fresh and cheerful against the bright green foliage.*

*Above: Mulleins, with their tall spires of intense yellow flowers, will really stand out in a border. They are a traditional favourite for cottage gardens.*

37

## PINK

A wide range of different qualities are included in the spectrum of pinks. We usually think of it as a soft colour with romantic connotations, but there are some shades that are positively startling. This is particularly so towards the red end of its range where it starts to merge with magenta and cerise. There are a number of popular annuals in the colour sometimes described as shocking pink, such as busy Lizzies, petunias, geraniums and cosmos. At the other end of the range there are pinks that are so soft they are no more than a blushed white. These can be very delicate.

*Above: This evening primrose has flowers of a delicate pale pink. With its sprawling habit, it works beautifully in an informal setting.*

*Above: Semperflorens begonias are among the most versatile annuals. This pink variety will flower right through to the end of autumn.*

### Soft Colours

The paler shades of pink can be very romantic, especially when combined with other soft pastels such as blues, lavenders and mauves. These can be used in an informal border to produce a haze of colours that merge into one another, rather than a distinct band of colour. Some of the very pale flowers open white and gradually turn pink, or fade to white with age – these are especially good for producing a mingling of tones. Pale pastels, while less striking than the brighter reds, will shine out more clearly in the evening twilight, or in dull, overcast weather.

*Above: Several shades of pink can be combined together successfully. This works either in a formal setting or when the colours are mixed together as here.*

## Where to Use Pinks

Pinks are useful in all kinds of different settings. In containers or bedding schemes, the stronger tones work well in combination with blue and white, and almost any shade of pink looks good with silver-leaved plants. For a really dramatic effect, try a bright pink together with red or orange. The softer pinks are best in an informal border, particularly with other pale and delicate flowers. This kind of combination can also be very successful in containers – the effect may not be as striking, but you can almost create a cottage garden in miniature.

*Above: This band of busy Lizzies, by using a mixture of different pinks and white, edged with silver foliage, produces a soft effect yet still looks neat and formal.*

39

### Pinks in the Shade

All the different pinks can look good in a shady position. The paler tones in particular will stand out very well. Unfortunately, as with most of the other colours of annual, not many pink-flowered plants will grow successfully in these conditions. Reliable busy Lizzies and Semperflorens begonias, however, do come in a very extensive range of pinks. They work especially well in containers – a large pot of busy Lizzies will make a mound of solid long-lasting colour, and in a hanging basket it can form a ball with a similar effect.

*Above: This geranium is named Pelargonium 'Apple Blossom Rosebud', no doubt because of the distinctive pink blush on the outer petals.*

*Above: The large, bold flowers of dahlias are sure to impress. They are a popular choice for flower arranging.*

POPULAR PINK ANNUALS

*Alcea rosea* 'Rose'
*Antirrhinum majus*
(numerous varieties)
*Centaurea cyanus* (pink forms)
*Diascia* (numerous varieties)
*Dianthus* (numerous varieties)
*Godetia grandiflora* 'Satin Pink'
*Helichrysum bracteatum* 'Rose'
*Impatiens* Impact Rose
*Lathyrus odoratus*
(numerous varieties)
*Lavatera trimestris* 'Mont Rose'
*Nicotiana* 'Domino Salmon-Pink'
*Nigella damascena*
'Miss Jekyll Pink'
*Papaver somniferum*
*Pelargonium* (numerous varieties)
*Petunia* (numerous varieties)
Semperflorens begonias

## Qualities of Colour

The effect produced by pinks can vary depending on a number of factors. Plants that have large flowers, or are covered in a mass of blooms, obviously make a powerful impact. Flowers with a solid, uniform colour, such as busy Lizzies and many geraniums and dahlias, also appear more intensely pink than those with tones shading from darker to lighter, such as sweet peas, daisies and pink Californian poppies. Texture also plays a part: the satiny sheen of some poppies and mallows creates a lighter feel than the rich, velvety softness of petunias, for example. Even the shape makes a difference: an open, round flower seems to make a more direct statement than a curiously shaped one such as a sweet pea.

*Above: The pale pink of this geranium is blotched with a deep purplish pink, producing a softer, more delicate effect than a single colour.*

*Above: The petals of opium poppies, with their characteristic dark spots at the centre, have an exquisite satiny texture.*

41

## BLUE AND LAVENDER

True blue is less easy to find in flowers than most of the other colours, and gardeners tend to include lavender within the definition of blue. Often a plant will have 'blue' in its name when this seems almost wishful thinking on the part of the breeders. However, there are some outstanding pure blue flowers, and these are highly prized. Lobelias are one of the best among the annuals, with both pale and deep blue varieties, and a long flowering season. Felicias are another useful blue flower for containers. In borders, love-in-a-mist and forget-me-nots, though flowering more briefly, are beautiful while they last.

*Above:* Love-in-a-mist, with its exquisite feathery foliage, is one of the prettiest of the cottage garden plants. It will self-sow profusely, and blends in well with any informal scheme.

*Above:* Echiums provide blues over a long period as the spirals of buds gradually unfold, introducing a constant display of deep or light blue flowers, usually offset by touches of pink.

### ROMANTIC BLUE ANNUALS

*Ageratum houstonianum*
*Borago officinalis*
*Brachycome iberidifolia*
*Campanula medium*
*Centaurea cyanus*
*Cynoglossum amabile*
*Echium* 'Blue Bedder'
*Echium vulgare*
*Felicia bergeriana*
*Gilia*
*Godetia bottae* 'Lady in Blue'
*Lathyrus odoratus* (various varieties)
*Legousia pentagonica*
*Limonium sinuatum* 'Azure'
*Limonium sinuatum* 'Blue Bonnet'
*Linanthus liniflorus*
*Lobelia erinus*
*Myosotis*
*Nemophila menziesii*
*Nigella damascena*
*Nolana paradoxa* 'Blue Bird'
*Petunia*
*Primula* (blue varieties)
*Salvia farinacea* 'Victoria'
*Viola x wittrockiana*

## Moody Blues

The expression 'the blues' means sadness, and it is easy to see how this idea came about, particularly when we compare it to the phrase 'seeing red', describing anger. Fortunately, however, this does not mean that a garden full of red flowers will make us angry, or that blue flowers will bring on a fit of depression. The emotional qualities of colours inevitably have a negative side, but this need not worry gardeners unduly, since the beauty of plants and flowers counteracts any of these possible negative effects. So just as red, the hottest colour in the spectrum, can induce energy and vitality, blue, at the coolest end, can have a wonderfully calming, soothing effect. Place blues where you have a seat so that they will encourage a feeling of relaxation.

*Above: The delicate flowers of baby blue-eyes* (Nemophila menziesii) *combine white and pure soft blue in a very appealing way.*

*Above:* Cerinthe major *has bright blue flowers that contrast strikingly with the blooms of* Helianthemum *'Apricot'.*

43

## Combining with Blue

Perhaps because of its subdued nature, blue can combine happily with virtually any other colour, though the effects will be very different. You can create a peaceful, dreamy haze of colour by mixing soft blues with shades of lavender and violet, particularly when delicate, feathery plants such as love-in-a-mist are included, or even the delightful blue morning glory climbing up a trellis behind. However, this combination can become dull, and is perhaps best confined to small areas or containers. In an informal bed, these muted tones can be lifted by touches of white, cream or pale pink.

*Above: The wonderfully named shoo-fly flower is produced on a large bushy plant that fits in well in mixed borders. The blue is set off against the green of the leaves and black of the stems.*

*Above: Cornflowers are among the most intensely blue annuals. They are excellent in informal beds, as well as in a wildflower garden.*

Blue and white, perhaps with trailing gypsophila, is also effective in containers, and alternate clumps of blue lobelia and white alyssum were once almost obligatory as edging for bedding schemes. Formal bedding and containers can also look stunning with blue and red or orange, or all three together. In a less formal setting, try morning glories with nasturtiums in shades of orange and yellow.

A somewhat cooler effect, though still quite striking, can be created with blue and yellow – the mood will vary depending whether you choose fresh, pale yellows or the warmer golds. You

could even include some of the blue
flowers with yellow centres, like the
dramatic *Convolvulus tricolor*.

### Blue in the Shade

There are not many blue annuals that
will grow well in the shade, and the
colour does not stand out very clearly
in low light. Lobelia will tolerate partial shade, however, and forget-me-nots
and pansies will also flower if the
shade is not too deep. The paler blues
tend to show up more effectively, and
can look charming in containers, combined with almost any other colour.

*Above: Blue can sometimes act as a
background colour, as here where it
allows the peachy-coloured dahlias to be
picked out.*

*Above: Lobelia is one of the most useful blue flowers. Here it is combined with white
flowers to create a delightful edging to a border.*

## VIOLET AND PURPLE

Blue with a little red added makes violet, and increasing the proportion of red brings it to purple. Violet can be deep, intense and glowing, and as it moves towards purple the colour becomes warmer and more friendly. It is easy to see why these colours have often been associated with royalty and high status, as they have a rich, opulent quality, particularly the deeper shades. They make a strong statement wherever they are used. The paler shades of purple, moving towards pink, are more unobtrusive and work well in any informal combination, giving a softer appearance.

*Above: The floss flower can produce a soft, cloudlike mass of colour, and is excellent for bedding. It comes in a range of blues, purples, pinks and white.*

*Above:* Silene armeria *'Electra' forms a sheet of magenta-purple flowers for a short season in summer.*

### VIOLET AND PURPLE ANNUALS

Antirrhinum 'Purple King'
Callistephus chinensis
(purple and violet varieties)
Centaurea cyanus 'Black Ball'
Cleome spinosa 'Violet Queen'
Eschscholzia californica
'Purple-Violet'
Eustoma grandiflora
Heliotropium
Hesperis matronalis
Impatiens (purple varieties)
Limonium sinuatum 'Midnight' or
'Purple Monarch'
Lunaria annua
Malva sylvestris subsp. mauritanica
Orychiophragmus violaceus
Papaver somniferum
(purple varieties)
Petunia (purple varieties)

### Combining with Violet

The rich yet subtle qualities of violet make it a difficult colour to combine, though used with care it can be highly effective. White is always a safe choice, and together with blues, lavenders and cream this can make a lovely soft combination. Violet teamed with red or orange is much more striking, being on opposite sides of the colour wheel, but can have a very pleasing effect in a container or formal bed. Yellow with violet can also work, though some might find the effect too garish – you will need to experiment carefully to see whether the pale yellows or the warmer golds suit your taste. Adding white to the scheme can help make this combination easier on the eye.

*Above: The yellow centres of purple cosmos flowers give it a bright, cheerful look, quite different from purple alone. It needs a sunny position to flower well.*

*Above:* Ipomoea indica *has rich purple trumpet-shaped flowers. It is a tender climber and in a hot summer can reach a height of 6m (20ft).*

47

## Combining with Purple

The warm tones of purple combine well with most other colours, though as with the violets, care needs to be taken with yellow, as the results may not be to everyone's taste. Purples work well in an informal border or container, perhaps mixed with blues, pinks and white, or in a more random mixture of many different colours. Some annuals are sold in mixed colours, for example old-fashioned sweet peas and snapdragons, and

*Left: The biennial galactites has soft, feathery, thistle-like purple flowers. The delicate leaves, with their silvery markings, are equally attractive but very prickly.*

*Above: The Swan River daisy has small flowers with very finely cut petals. This creates a wonderful hazy effect which works well in contrast to more solid colours.*

*Above:* Purple-flowered beans can be as decorative in the flower garden as they are in the vegetable patch. Some produce purple pods as an added bonus.

these often include shades of purple which blend with the other colours in a very pleasing way.

## Purple in the Shade

The deeper violets and purples do not show up particularly well in the shade, but the lighter tones can look very good. Honesty, busy Lizzies, pansies and lobelias all come in purple varieties, and these will tolerate moderate shade.

*Right:* The ever-popular petunias produce showy flowers in a wide range of colours, including this rich mauve.

## WHITE AND CREAM

These are two favourite colours in the garden, and not only because of their adaptability in combining with other colours. White is generally associated with purity, tranquillity and spirituality, qualities we often seek in a garden. When white flowers are contrasted with deep green foliage they show up beautifully, allowing every detail of the flowers to be seen. Paler or silvery foliage gives a more delicate effect, enhancing the feeling of purity.

White can be used very effectively on its own, to create an all-white border, with a very calm, peaceful quality. However, flowers are very rarely a

*Above: This marigold,* Tagetes *'French Vanilla', is a rich shade of cream. Marigolds come in many colours, from cream to yellow and orange, which all blend well together.*

***Above:*** *Many blue and purple flowers also produce a white form. The white foxglove is excellent in white borders, and is also good for cutting.*

completely pure white – a white that is tinged with green or blue will have a cool quality that is quite different from a pinkish or creamy white. When different white flowers are combined together, these subtle variations become more noticeable, so you need to choose your plants with care if you want to create a unified effect.

Cream is a white that has been softened by the slightest hint of yellow. This makes it less harsh and turns it into a romantic colour that can be combined with other soft, pastel colours to create a hazy atmosphere.

## Combining White and Cream

It is almost impossible to go wrong when combining white with other colours. The stark contrast with bright reds and oranges, or with strong blues, can give a very clean, neat look in a formal bedding scheme. White teamed with yellow, particularly the paler yellows, has a fresh, springlike feel and works well in any situation – a container or even an entire border devoted to yellow and white can look stunning. White and cream both go well with soft pastel pinks and blues – cream is particularly good for creating an old-fashioned cottage garden feel. The warmer whites, verging towards cream or pink, may blend in more easily here.

*Above: Candytuft is a traditional cottage garden plant, producing a soft mass of white or pink flowers. The neater-growing forms are also good in more formal bedding schemes.*

*Above:* Osteospermum *'Prostratum' produces one of the whitest flowers imaginable. In the sunlight, they can look positively dazzling.*

*Above: Gypsophila, with its delicate wiry stems, can produce a soft billowing cloud of white flowers when planted en masse. It is also perfect for bouquets.*

## White in the Shade

For brightening up a shady spot, white is the ideal colour, as it shines out far more clearly than darker colours. Indeed, it is almost more effective here than in bright sunlight, where it can be bleached out and lost among the stronger colours in the garden. As always, the difficulty is in finding plants that will thrive in these conditions. Honesty has a white-flowered form, with attractive shiny seed-cases after the flowers are over. There are also white forms of busy Lizzies, Semperflorens begonias, pansies and lobelias, and these are excellent for containers.

## Whites for Cutting

All colours of annuals are suitable for cutting, but the white varieties are most in demand – large quantities are used for weddings and church decoration, and they are also popular for all types of flower arranging. A number of the tender perennials are perfect for this, such as chrysanthemums and dahlias, which can look magnificent in a large, formal arrangement. The tiny floating flowers of gypsophila will give a touch of airiness to the display, while carnations will add that vital ingredient, scent. Cosmos and eustoma will add solidity and the white foxglove height.

*Above: White flowers are perfect for illuminating dark corners. Busy Lizzies are particularly useful for this.*

*Above:* A terracotta window box is a perfect foil to this simple yet effective combination of white Nicotiana and Heliotropium.

*Above:* White Dahlia *'Kenora Challenger'* always looks impressive, whether growing in a border or used in flower arrangements.

## SOFT WHITE ANNUALS

*Anoda cristata* 'Silver Cup'
*Clarkia pulchella* 'Snowflake'
*Cleome spinosa* 'Helen Campbell'
*Cosmos bipinnatus* 'Purity'
*Digitalis purpurea* f. *albiflora*
*Gypsophila elegans* 'Covent Garden'
*Helianthus annuus* 'Italian White'
*Hibiscus trionum*
*Impatiens* Tempo White
*Lathyrus odoratus* (various varieties)
*Lavatera trimestris* 'Mont Blanc'
*Limonium sinuatum* 'Iceberg'
*Lunaria annua* var. *albiflora*
*Malope trifida* 'Alba'
*Malope trifida* 'White Queen'
*Nemesia* 'Mello White'
*Nemophila maculata*
*Nicotiana sylvestris*
*Nigella damascena* 'Miss Jekyll Alba'
*Osteospermum* 'Glistening White'
*Papaver somniferum*
(various varieties)
*Pelargonium* (various varieties)

## MIXED COLOURS

Designing colour schemes can seem complicated enough with flowers of one colour, but a further dimension is added by the fact that many flowers are made up of more than one colour. Sometimes there are separate bands or an intricate pattern of distinct colours, sometimes the colours fuse into one another. Often there is a base colour which is overlaid with a pattern in one or more different colours.

There are also a number of annuals, particularly old-fashioned varieties, that are sold in mixtures of different colours. Almost all annuals of more than one colour may be sold in this way.

*Above: The gold and deep burnt orange petals of this sunflower give a dramatic, flame-like effect.*

*Above: The flowers of this petunia have a gradual deepening of colour towards the centre.*

### Patterned Flowers

Flowers that contain more than one colour can produce very different effects. French marigolds sometimes have a dramatic pattern of gold or orange and deep mahogany, and *Convolvulus tricolor*, with its blue, yellow and white trumpets, can look quite startling. Carnations are often more delicate, with a narrow dark band around the edge – even those with bolder markings tend to be in toning colours. The blue flowers of forget-me-nots, with their white centres, can give the effect of being a paler shade of blue.

## Mixed Batches

Most of the flowers that are sold as mixed will be within a limited range of colours. Nasturtiums, Californian poppies and marigolds will come in oranges, yellows and cream. Snapdragons and toadflax have a wider colour range, including pink, purple, red, white and yellow. Sweet peas come in soft shades of pink, purple and white.

## A Riot of Colour

Flowers that are sold in mixed batches are not generally very useful for formal schemes, where the colours need to be uniform and predictable. In mixed beds and containers, however, they can be easier to blend in than flowers of a single colour. As the different colours in the mixture usually harmonize well with each other, an informal, relaxed look is immediately created, gentler on the eye than a block of one colour, yet still with a softly unified effect.

---

### MIXED-COLOURED ANNUALS

*Dianthus barbatus*
*Dianthus chinensis*
*Nemesia*
*Primula*
*Salpiglossis*
*Schizanthus*
*Tagetes*
*Viola* x *wittrockiana*

---

*Above: Violas come in mixtures including lavender and cream, and sometimes a darker violet, all with delicate markings on the petals.*

## FOLIAGE

When we think of plants, we naturally think first of flowers, but foliage has an equally important part to play. Whether we treat it merely as background or give it a starring role, it goes a long way to determining the overall look of the garden.

### Leaf Colour

Most leaves are green, because of the chlorophyll they need to survive, but this can range from bright lime or softest silvery-grey to almost black. Then there are deep purples and reds, golden, yellow, silver and even grey-blue. Variegated leaves can be patterned with almost any combination of these.

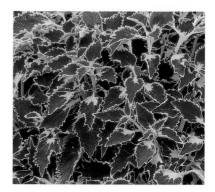

*Above: The glorious carpet foliage of maroon and lime-green* Solenostemon *'Glory of Luxembourg'.*

### Leaf Shape and Texture

There is as much variation here as there is with colour, and great effects can be produced. The large serrated leaves of melianthus make a striking contrast with smaller, rounded leaves. Then there are soft, velvety plants such as *Helichrysum petiolare*, which looks especially good trailing down from hanging baskets. Another dimension is added by grasses, with their tall, slender elegance. Though they are grown mainly for their stems and foliage, many have the added bonus of attractive flowerheads, which can last for a long period.

*Above: A perfect plant for mixed borders, red orache produces beautiful deep purple foliage, with the added bonus that it can make a colourful ingredient in salads.*

---

### ANNUALS FOR FOLIAGE

*Brassica oleracea*
*Canna*
*Coleus blumei*
*Euphorbia marginata*
*Galactites tomentosa*
*Helichrysum petiolare*
*Ocimum basilicum* 'Purple Ruffles'

---

## Using Foliage

It is quite possible to create a scheme, either in a formal bed or in a container, using entirely foliage, and this can be an excellent way of displaying the different colours and forms. Generally, however, it is used alongside flowers. Plants with attractive foliage can be used in containers or beds to help link the colours of the flowers, or to soften the overall effect. Plants with brightly coloured foliage, such as coleus, can continue the colour theme of the flowers.

*Above: The soft, feathery flowerheads of this squirrel tail grass* (Hordeum jubatum) *are at their most effective when caught in the sunlight.*

*Above:* Helichrysum petiolare, *with its soft grey, rounded leaves, provides a good foil to all kinds of flowers. Its trailing habit makes it perfect for containers, especially hanging baskets, and it is also an attractive addition to bouquets.*

| ANNUAL GRASSES |
| :---: |
| *Agrostis nebulosa* |
| *Briza maxima* |
| *Chloris barbata* |
| *Hordeum jubatum* |
| *Lagurus ovatus* |
| *Panicum miliaceum* |
| *Tricholaena rosea* |

# Colourful Annuals at a Glance

THIS QUICK REFERENCE SECTION CAN BE USED TO HELP SELECT THE MOST SUITABLE ANNUALS FOR A VARIETY OF DIFFERENT PURPOSES AND CONDITIONS. IT INCLUDES ANNUALS AND BIENNIALS AS WELL AS TENDER AND SHORT-LIVED PERENNIALS THAT ARE USED AS ANNUALS.

| Plant Name | Height | Flower Colour |
|---|---|---|
| *Ageratum* HH/A or B b (t) C | up to 30cm (12in) | blue, pink and white |
| *Alonsoa* HH/A b t hb w C | up to 45cm (18in) | scarlet and orange |
| *Amaranthus* HH/A b mb C S | up to 1.5m (5ft) | red-purple |
| *Antirrhinum* H or HH/SP b t mb C | up to 45cm (18in) | wide range (not blue) |
| *Arctotis* HH/A or TP b C | up to 60cm (2ft) | most colours except blue |
| *Argemone* HH/A b mb C F | up to 1m (3ft) | white and yellow |
| *Argyranthemum* TP b mb t hb w C | up to 60cm (2ft) | pink and yellow |
| *Atriplex* H/A b mb F | up to 1.2m (4ft) | foliage red |
| *Begonia* Semperflorens TP ps/s b t hb w C | up to 15cm (6in) | white, pink, orange, red and yellow |
| *Bidens ferulifolia* HH/SP b t hb w C | up to 90cm (3ft) | yellow |
| *Borago officinalis* HH/A b C F He | 90cm (3ft) | blue and white |
| *Brachycome iberidifolia* H/A b t hb w C | 23cm (9in) | blue, pink and white |
| *Calceolaria* HH/A b t hb w C | up to 30cm (12in) | yellow and orange |
| *Calendula officinalis* H/A b C He | 45cm (18in) | orange, yellow and cream |
| *Callistephus chinensis* HH/A b t C Sc | up to 60cm (2ft) | all colours |
| *Canna* TP b mb C F | up to 1.5m (5ft) | orange and red, purple foliage (some) |
| *Centaurea cyanus* H/A b C | 60cm (2ft) | blue, pink and white |
| *Cerinthe major* H/A b t C | 30cm (12in) | purple flowers, grey foliage |
| *Cheiranthus cheiri* H/B b (t) mb C Sc | 45cm (18in) | orange, yellow and red |

Calceolaria

Lathyrus odoratus

| | | |
|---|---|---|
| *Chrysanthemum* TP b t w C Sc Cu | 1.2m (4ft) | all except true blue |
| *Clarkia* HH/A b t hb w C | up to 50cm (20in) | pink, red and mauve |
| *Cleome* HH/A b mb C S | up to 1.2m (4ft) | pink, white and purple |
| *Collinsia* H/A b tolerates ps C | up to 30cm (12in) | bicoloured in pink and purple |
| *Consolida* HH/A b (t) C | up to 45cm (18in) | blue, white, pink and purple |
| *Convolvulus tricolor* HH/A b hb C | up to 30cm (12in) | tricoloured mainly blue with white and yellow |
| *Coreopsis tinctoria* H/A b (t) C | up to 1.2m (4ft) | yellow, red, purple and brown forms |
| *Cosmos* HH or H/A b mb C | 90cm (3ft) | red, pink and white |
| *Dahlia* TP b C Cu | 1.2m (4ft) | all colours except true blue |
| *Dianthus chinensis* H/A b (t) mb e C | up to 23cm (9in) | pink, red and white |
| *Echium* H/A or B b t w C | up to 60cm (2ft) | blue, purple and pink |
| *Eschscholzia* H | up to 15cm (6in) | orange, cream and yellow |
| *Eustoma grandiflorus* T/A or B b C | up to 45cm (18in) | blue, purple, pink and white |
| *Felicia* HH/A b t hb w C | up to 60cm (2ft) | blue and white |
| *Gomphrena globosa* T/A b C | up to 60cm (2ft) | red, pink, purple and white |
| *Helianthus* H/A b C S | up to 2.5m (8ft) | yellow |
| *Helichrysum* HH/A or TP b t hb w C F | up to 60cm (2ft) | white, pink and yellow |
| *Heliotropium* HH/A b (t w) C Sc | 45cm (18in) | violet |
| *Hesperis matronalis* H/B b mb C Sc | 1.2m (4ft) | mauve and white |
| *Hordeum jubatum* H/A grass b C S | up to 45cm (18in) | |
| *Iberis* H/A b e t C | up to 30cm (12in) | white and pink |
| *Impatiens* TP b t hb w tolerates ps C | up to 30cm (12in) | red, orange, purple, pink and white |
| *Ipomoea* T/A b C | up to 5m (15ft) climber | blue, pink, purple and red |
| *Isatis tinctoria* H/B b C He | up to 1.2m (4ft) | yellow |
| *Lathyrus odoratus* H/A b C Sc Cu | up to 1.8m (6ft) climber | red, pink, mauve and white |
| *Lavatera trimestris* H/A b C | up to 1.2m (4ft) | pink and white |
| *Limnanthes douglasii* H/A b e C Be | 15cm (6in) | bicoloured yellow and white |

Dahlia

Hesperis matronalis

| | | |
|---|---|---|
| *Linum grandiflorum* H/A b mb C | up to 75cm (30in) | red |
| *Lobelia erinus* HH/A b e t hb w C | up to 15cm (6in) some trailing | blue, purple and white |
| *Lobularia maritima* H/A b e t hb w C | 15cm (6in) | white and pink |
| *Lunaria annua* H/B b tolerates sh Sp C F | up to 1m (3ft) | purple and white, also variegated foliage forms |
| *Matthiola* HH or H/A b t C Sc | up to 45cm (18in) | pink, mauve and white |
| *Melianthus* TP b mb F C S | up to 3m (10ft) | red, foliage silver |
| *Moluccella laevis* HH/A b C | up to 1m (3ft) | green |
| *Myosotis* H/A b t hb w mb tolerates ps C | up to 30cm (12in) | blue |
| *Nemesia* HH/A b t hb w C | up to 30cm (12in) | white, blue, yellow and purple |
| *Nicandra physalodes* H/A b C F | up to 1m (3ft) | blue |
| *Nicotiana* HH/A b t hb w C Sc (some) | up to 2.1m (7ft) | white and pink |
| *Nigella* H/A b mb C | 60cm (2ft) | blue and white |
| *Oenothera* H/B b mb C Sc | 90cm (3ft) | yellow, orange and pink (in evening) |
| *Omphalodes linifolia* H/A b mb C | up to 25cm (10in) | white |
| *Papaver* H/A b mb C | up to 90cm (3ft) | red, mauve, pink and white |
| *Pelargonium* TP b t w C F Sc (some) | up to 75cm (30in) some trailing | red, pink and white, some scented foliage |
| *Petunia* HH/SP b t hb w C Sc (some) | 25cm (10in) | all colours |
| *Phacelia* H/A b C | up to 50cm (20in) | blue, lavender and white |
| *Phlox drummondii* HH/A b (t) C | up to 45cm (18in) | purple, pale blue, pink and white |
| *Portulaca* HH/A b C | up to 20cm (8in) | most colours |
| *Ricinus* HH/A b F | up to 3m (10ft) | red, foliage red and bronze |
| *Rudbeckia* HH/A b mb C | up to 1m (3ft) | yellow, gold, orange-red and brown |
| *Salpiglossis* HH/A b t C | up to 60cm (2ft) | most colours |
| *Salvia farinacea* HH/SP b mb hb t w C | up to 38cm (15in) | scarlet, blue, pink and purple |

Lunaria annua

Impatiens

| *Salvia splendens* HH/SP b mb hb t w C | up to 38cm (15in) | scarlet, blue and pink |
|---|---|---|
| *Salvia viridis* HH/A b mb hb t w C | up to 38cm (15in) | scarlet, blue and purple |
| *Sanvitalia* H/A b t hb w C | up to 20cm (8in) creeping | yellow |
| *Senecio cineraria* (*S. maritima*) TS b t hb w F | up to 60cm (2ft) | flowers yellow, foliage silver |
| *Silybum marianum* H/B mb F | up to 75cm (30in) | flowers purple, white-veined leaves |
| *Tagetes* HH/A b t hb w C | up to 30cm (12in) | yellow and orange |
| *Tithonia* HH/A b mb C | up to 1.2m (4ft) | orange |
| *Tropaeolum majus* H/A b (t) C | up to 90cm (3ft) climber | orange, red and yellow |
| *Verbascum* H/B b mb S C F | up to 2m (7ft) | yellow |
| *Verbena* x *hybrida* TP b hb mb t w C | up to 30cm (12in) | red, purple, pink and white |
| *Viola* x *wittrockiana* H/SP b hb mb t w tolerates ps C | 25cm (10in) | all colours |

### KEY TO SYMBOLS

Unless otherwise stated the plants all prefer a sunny position

H = Hardy
HH = Half-hardy
T = Tender
TS = Tender Shrub
A = Annual
B = Biennial
SP = Short-lived Perennial
TP = Tender Perennial
b = beds
e = edging
hb = hanging baskets
mb = mixed borders
t = tubs

(t) = mainly used in beds but some could be used in tubs, pots or similar containers
w = window boxes
ps = partial shade
sh = shade
Be = Grown to attract Bees
C = Grown for Colour
Cu = Grown for Cutting
F = Grown for Foliage
He = Grown as Herb
S = Grown for Shape
Sc = Grown for Scent
Sp = Grown for Seed Pods

Verbena

Tagetes

# Common Names of Annuals

Plants where the botanical and the common name are the same, such as Chrysanthemum, have been omitted.

African daisy *Arctotis*
African marigold *Tagetes erecta*
baby blue-eyes *Nemophila menziesii*
bells of Ireland *Moluccella laevis*
black-eyed Susan *Rudbeckia*
blue daisy *Felicia*
borage *Borago officinalis*
busy Lizzie *Impatiens*
Californian poppy *Eschscholzia*

*Above: Sunflowers and nasturtiums.*

castor oil plant *Ricinus*
cherry pie *Heliotropum*
China aster *Callistephus chinensis*
Chinese pink *Dianthus chinensis*
cineraria *Senecio cineraria*
coneflower *Echinacea*
cornflower *Centaurea cyanus*
creeping zinnia *Sanvitalia*
dame's violet *Hesperis matronalis*
evening primrose *Oenothera biennis*
floss flower *Ageratum*
flowering flax *Linum grandiflorum*
forget-me-not *Myosotis*
French marigold *Tagetes patula*
geranium *Pelargonium*
globe amaranth *Gomphrena globosa*
godetia *Clarkia*
honesty *Lunaria annua*

honey bush *Melianthus*
honeywort *Cerinthe major*
larkspur *Consolida*
love-in-a-mist *Nigella*
love-lies-bleeding *Amaranthus*
mask flower *Alonsoa*
Mexican sunflower *Tithonia*
milk thistle *Silybum marianum*
morning glory *Ipomoea*
mullein *Verbascum*
nasturtium *Tropaeolum*
pansy *Viola* x *wittrockiana*
poached-egg flower *Limnanthes douglasii*
poppy *Papaver*
pot marigold *Calendula officinalis*
prickly poppy *Argemone*
purslane *Portulaca*
red orache *Atriplex*
scorpion weed *Phacelia*
shoo-fly flower *Nicandra physalodes*

slipper flower *Calceolaria*
snapdragon *Antirrhinum*
spiderflower *Cleome*
squirrel tail grass *Hordeum jubatum*
stock *Matthiola*
sunflower *Helianthus*
Swan River daisy *Brachycome iberidifolia*
sweet alyssum *Lobularia maritima*
sweet pea *Lathyrus odoratus*
sweet rocket *Hesperis matronalis*
Texan bluebell *Eustoma grandiflorus*
tickseed *Coreopsis tinctoria*
toadflax *Linaria*
Venus' navelwort *Omphalodes linifolia*
wallflower *Cheiranthus cheiri*
woad *Isatis tinctoria*

# Index

***Above:*** Pelargonium *'Lass O'Gowrie'.*

# Index

**Above:** *Glowing orange-red dahlias.*